MeNU
SPECIAL
frog soup

This book is dedicated to all the frogs
who made the leap before they became soup.

Just <u>don't</u> be a sh*t boss!

Written and illustrated by Tenille Dowe
Copyright © 2025 Tenille Dowe

First Printing, 2025
Published by Creative Heart Connection
www.creativeheartconnection.com

ISBN 978-1-7641624-3-2

Just don't be a sh*t boss!

A guide on how NOT to be an @R$*h0<3!

Written and Illustrated
by Tenille Dowe

In a pond that was sparkling,
so fresh and so bright,
a little green frog sat
and dreamed about his passion and
purpose with all of his might.

He dreamed of adventure,
of purpose, of cheer,
but whispers of trouble
soon started to near.

Just don't be a sh*t boss!

the frog softly said,
as visions of teamwork danced
round in his head.

He pictured a leader both
fair and sincere,
but chaos was coming...
it crept ever near.

He looked up to the branches of the
tall, towering gums,
where whispers were hushed and
the chatter just hummed.

The animals were all around
with wide worried eyes,
all fearing the chaos they
knew lurked here in disguise.

At the first meeting,
the chaos and overload was clear.
Full of big rocks and
small rocks all tossed in the air.
"Oh, follow my vision!"
the lorikeet chirped with a grin.
Deadlines for most, but details were
tossed in the bin.
They talked and they squawked,
but no action was near.

Just <u>don't</u> be a sh*t boss!

the frog whispered low.
As meetings grew longer and
progress grew slow.
The rainbow lorikeet squawked
and chirped as she
tossed more and more rocks in.

SQUAWK

Each small and big rock,
a new burden to bear,
that never belonged to the frog's own chair.
She flung in a gem with a glittering gleam,
a sparkling distraction,
or a manipulative scheme?
The frog hoped for some order,
a plan or a chart,
but the rainbow lorikeet's antics
were tearing his hard work and effort apart.

The lorikeet watched him and
schemed with a grin.
She dangled a promise to lure him right in,
"A new pond for you, so shiny and sweet!"
The pond was a saucepan with barely a seat.
She chirped of cool waters
and shade from the heat,
while stirring in gossip,
like a poisonous treat.
For leaders who trick and spread rumours
for the goss, here's the golden rule:

Just <u>don't</u> be a sh*t boss!

The water was lukewarm at first,
a deceitful disguise.
She dropped in a gem,
a glittering prize,
then loaded up rocks till
they reached to the brim.....
The frog kept on working,
no rest, just to win.
He built new systems,
he patched every flaw,
met deadlines and targets
and obeyed every law.
Still blind to the tricks and the
colourful lies of the rainbow lorikeet
with the scheming eyes.

The lion, he never listened at all.
He strutted with pride and made the
lazy sloth feel so small.

He mocked and he sneered in a
loud, boastful and mean way.
The rainbow lorikeet blinked,
turning a blind eye each day.

Just don't be a sh*t boss!
the frog whispered near,
as meanness echoed that no one
would hear!

The lion was sooooo loud.
He loved the sound of his own voice!
He roared in every meeting
and gave no one's ears a choice.

He puffed out his chest in a prideful display,
while roaring through meetings,
no listening his way.
The sloth shrank in silence,
afraid and alone.
Bullied by power that
chilled to the bone.

Just _don't_ be a sh*t boss!
the frog gave a cheer!
As fear filled the pond and respect disappeared

ROAR

The kitten was playful,
with bright eager eyes.
She bounded with hope and
believed in the prize,
but the lion grew jealous
and bullied her with pride.

ROAR

Until the kitten felt broken
and hid far inside.

Just _don't_ be a sh*t boss!
the frog gave a sigh.
As kindness and
fairness was left
high and dry.

Perched high in her tall gum tree,
the rainbow lorikeet stayed.
With the power to hush what the
lion displayed.

The kitten sat trembling,
so small in her plea,
yet the lorikeet did nothing
and just watched on silently.

Doing nothing at all was her
leadership way.

The kitten grew weary,
her sparkle was gone.
She whispered to the frog,
"I can't keep hanging on"
The lorikeet squawked while
pretending to care
and sprinkled gossip
like seeds through the air.
Then came the big twist,
that made all jaws drop,
the sloth got promoted
for doing... a flop!

The frog watched it happen,
his heart feeling sore.
He'd leapt for adventure,
but was now stuck in a war.
The pond that seemed perfect
was murky and mean,
a toxic old swamp dressed
in shimmering blue and green.
The heat was turned up and
the flames burned so bright.
He knew he must leap
or be frog soup by night.

MeNU
SPECIAL
frog soup

Up in her gum tree the lorikeet sat,
bright feathers all shining,
while she had a chat.
Her flock gathered round for
the juiciest news and she served it up
fresh like scandalous frog stews.
"Oh, the frogs I have boiled!"
she cackled with glee,
*"Slow simmered in silence and they never
blamed me!"*
She bragged of her power,
her colourful reign,
while the environment below
groaned under the strain.

She whispered of sloths and
the kitten's lost zest.
She stirred up the drama
and gave it her best.
For leaders who gossip
and stir up the pot,
soon find their own feathers
in quite a tight knot.
Respect starts to vanish,
trust falls through the floor
and chaos comes knocking
with drama galore.
So here is the lesson for
bosses who lead,
don't gossip, don't whisper,
don't plant a bad seed.

Strong leaders bring sunlight,
not toxic and poisonous shade.
They foster and value teamwork
where trust can be made.
They lift up their jungle
and help all unite,
they seek out each strength
and guide talents to take flight.
Effective leadership builds trust,
not loss and if you forget.....

Just *don't* be
a sh*t boss!

Meanwhile, back with the frog....

The heat burned like melting lava,
the boiling water was a trap.
He saw through the lies and
the rainbow lorikeet's manipulative crap.
With courage and insight,
he sprang with a shout....

Just *don't* be a sh*t boss!

as he leapt right out.
He left all the chaos,
the swamp and the fight.
He dreamed of a pond that was
calm and was bright.

Frog paused for a moment
to breathe and be still,
to quiet his worries and
strengthen his will.
He knew he had value,
a courage profound and longed to find kindness,
where care could be found.
He whispered,
"This next leap must truly be right,"
and penned a poem with the lessons that
gave him reasons to fight.

Just don't be a sh*t boss!

By the Frog

Lorikeet sat in her gum tree so tall,
holding the power to fix it all.
Silence, she chose just sipping her tea,
while chaos boiled like a frog in misery.

They tossed tiny rocks to those they adored
and dumped heavy boulders on those ignored

The sloth moved slowly, bullied each day,
until Lorikeet crowned him "Qualified Hooray"
Promotion by pity, not skill or grit.
A jungle of nonsense, oh what a pile of sh*t!

The kitten once proud, in her fur of delight,
Lost her zest to toxins that poisoned her light.
Her voice grew smaller, her courage grew thin,
while Lorikeet watched with a colourful grin.

So, here are the lessons in rhyme and in cheer,
don't boil your frogs, don't roar in their ear,
share rocks with fairness, both big and small.
Strong leaders don't gossip
or spread lies and rumours at all.
Every leader should lead with kindness,
or don't lead at all.

So here is the lesson,
as simple as this....
If leading is something
you cannot dismiss,
then lead with
compassion, fairness
and care.
Not chaos and glitter
and inflated ego
and pride everywhere.

For ponds can turn toxic
and teams can go wrong,
when sh*t bosses chase sparkles,
roar loud and are not strong.
So, hear the refrain as you leap
to the top.....
Just don't be a sh*t boss!
and let the harm stop.

The frog now is thriving,
so happy and free.
He found a cool pond by
a jacaranda tree.

Bright scented blooms of
purples and pinks
cast shade all around.
A haven of calm,
where no stress can be found.

He smiles at the journey and sometimes
gets a nervous twitch, as he
remembers the lessons and the cost,
and whispers with hope
"Lead with kindness, not loss"

And always remember...

Just **don't** be a sh*t boss!

The End